EXTRAORDINARY
WEALTH

7 Simple Strategies for Business Owners

EXTRAORDINARY WEALTH

7 Simple Strategies for Business Owners

NIKHIL NAIK

Worldwide Published by
Pendown Press

PENDOWN PRESS
An ISO 9001 & ISO 14001 Certified Co.,
Regd. Office: 2525/193, 1st Floor, Onkar Nagar-A,
Tri Nagar, Delhi-110035
Ph.: 09350849407, 09312235086
E-mail: info@pendownpress.com
Branch Office: 1A/2A, 20, Hari Sadan, Ansari Road,
Daryaganj, New Delhi-110002
Ph.: 011-45794768
Website: PendownPress.com

First Edition: 2023

ISBN: 978-93-5554-614-2

Layout and Cover Designed by Pendown Graphics Team
Printed and Bound in India by Thomson Press India Ltd.

Contents

Introduction

I started my career in 1996, when I joined my father's business. Since then, I have met over 6,000 individuals from different backgrounds, religions, beliefs, financial states.. I have met those who are extremely well educated and those who don't have educational qualifications. In fact, one of our richest clients was someone who did not complete their high school.

These kinds of stories intrigued me. I was sure that these people were doing something right. I wanted to explore what that is. That was the inspiration for writing this book.

With my decades of experience in the investment and wealth management field, I always ask clients one question:

Do you want quick money or more money?

Invariably, they give the second answer. That's why this book is about creating more money, more wealth. And this has nothing to do with your income or how much profits your business is earning.

It is about changing the belief system about money and investments. Especially for first- and second-generation entrepreneurs.

So, what is this book about?

Will it tell you how to run your business as an entrepreneur? No.

Will it make you an expert about investment products? No.

Will it give you tips on how to get rich quickly? No.

Will it give you techniques on how to play the stock market? No.

Follow the journey of Sunil, who, with the help of his friend Nitin, is able to break the myths that surround entrepreneurship and money.

Because there is so much misinformation that surrounds the concepts of saving and investing. This creates confusion in the minds of those who are looking to grow their wealth.

I do not claim to know everything, but I can assure you that I have seen many things over the last couple of decades. I have seen everything from the 2008 crash to the tech bubble bursting. I have seen people going through painful cycles of buying real estate and not getting returns. I have seen people burning their fingers in futures and options and stock trading that's aimed at getting rich quickly.

As I share these stories, I promise to speak only from my experience.

In the following pages, I won't tell you what to do. I'll tell you what not to do.

I hope this book will set you on a successful path to creating and growing your wealth.

Nikhil Naik
Author

SECTION 1

Laying The Foundation

Reflection 1

The Pains of Being an Entrepreneur

08:00 AM

Sunil walked in the door of his Mumbai office. The vast open-plan space was empty. A huge modern chandelier twinkled in the sunlight. His glass-walled cabin was his safe space, with teak and marble interiors, art on the wall, a Turkish carpet.

He sank into his chair as his phone chimed with incoming emails. He was used to this. He had done a lot of hard work building up his family business over the last two decades. He was a second-generation entrepreneur, who had followed in his father's footsteps. It wasn't a planned career, but he was here, and he wasn't going anywhere.

09:00 AM

Sunil had Mr Ananth, an angry client, on the phone. A promised delivery had not reached them on time. This was one of Sunil's biggest, hard-won clients. His company could not delay things for them. A tense employee explained that there was a mix-up from their plant in Surat.

"Just because you don't know how to run your business properly, why must mine suffer," yelled Ananth. After many apologies, Sunil promised to meet him next week, and gave a new delivery date. Plus, a discount on their next order, which he could hardly afford to offer. Ananth agreed to the new conditions and said he could meet Sunil next Thursday. But there was a problem. That was the day he was to leave on a family vacation.

10:00 AM

"Can't make it to the trip - imp meeting on Thurs. You and kids go ahead," he texted his wife, Saumya. "You tell the kids. Also, reminder for annual day at Riya's school today @ 6," she replied. His daughter was singing a solo in the choir and would be very disappointed if he was not in the crowd.

He needed to focus and reorganise his calendar to make sure he could leave by 5.30 pm. It was a Thursday, and he knew he would be back here the next morning, and on Saturday as well. He could work on some of these projects then.

12:00 PM

After a hasty lunch at his desk, he had a staff meeting. A couple of employees asked for leave as they were planning to travel. Sunil gave permission, although he was slightly bitter about it. He kept thinking of the vacation he was missing out on. But the business was his. These employees, and his own livelihood, depended on it. He didn't have a choice.

04:00 PM

Next, his chartered accountant dropped in for a serious discussion. More funds were needed for the business. They were still suffering from the after-effects of Covid, which had hit their industry hard. Cash flow had seen a major crunch. Sunil would have to liquidate some of his investments.

He also brought up the fact that working with cash transactions was not helping Sunil or his business in the current day and age. But his customers and suppliers preferred to deal in cash. Banks and other financial institutions didn't take him seriously and would not give him real estate loans. It was not a good space to be in.

05:45 PM

Most of the staff had left. Sunil rushed out the office door, remembering that his driver was not available that evening. He had a fairly new Mercedes-Benz Maybach S580 which he had driven only a few times. He hadn't had time to explore all the capabilities. So, he was pleasantly surprised when he accidentally turned on the massage option on the driver's seat. It was badly needed after the day he had had so far!

06:30 PM

He reached the school auditorium by 6.30 pm. His wife, Saumya, and son, Ishan, had saved him a seat. But Riya had finished singing by then, and the program had moved on to the next act. "I tried," he told himself. Although it didn't make him feel any better.

Riya was of course upset. But she was in a better mood once he said sorry many times and stopped for dinner at her favourite restaurant. Sunil replied to emails from his phone as they chatted. His son was applying to universities abroad, and they had plenty to discuss. When it came down to the fees, he was not too worried. He had the cash.

09:30 PM

Sunil's Apple Watch reminded him to stand up and move around for a minute. He was in his home office, sending emails, assigning tasks, going over the numbers for the company. He took the moment to think of all that he had done today. Not achieved, just done. Nothing was linear about his day. He had spent the whole day firefighting one problem after another, be it professional or personal.

It reminded him of the definition of an entrepreneur he had once read: "His customers think he charges too much; his employees think he pays too less; his family thinks he earns nothing; and the government thinks he hides everything." It couldn't be truer in Sunil's case.

10:45 PM

Sunil also couldn't get the cash flow problem out of his mind. He had to figure out a solution, and fast. In bed, he mindlessly scrolled through YouTube, when an interview of Bollywood actor Abhishek Bachchan came up.

He had shared how his father, veteran actor Amitabh Bachchan, dealt with a similar issue. He had no active income.

So, he went out, asked for work from his industry friends, including producer and director Yash Chopra. The result: his comeback film, *Mohabbatein.*[1]

"Who could be Yash Chopra for me," wondered Sunil.

11:15 PM

The only person who Sunil could think of was Nitin. A fellow businessman, Nitin had built his company from the ground up.

He sent him a quick text: "Free to meet for a drink tomorrow?"

"I only drink on the weekends - let's make it Saturday? The usual place at 8," replied Nitin.

Sunil gladly agreed with a 'thumbs-up' emoji. He was determined not to give up, He would take action instead. As he thought of various ways he could fix his issues, he drifted off into sleep just as the clock struck midnight...

NOTES:

"Why?" Vs "Why Me?"

Do you often get caught up in doing small, mundane, unimportant tasks? Are urgent and important things left undone? Try out the **5 Whys method.**

Put down your problem statement, then start by asking why it's an issue. Once you figure out the reason behind that, ask why that reason exists. And so on. By the fifth "why", you usually reach the root cause of the problem.

Then, it's time for action. Put down what needs to be done. Give yourself a deadline. Break down and assign the tasks. And see what a difference it makes.

Here's a sample from Sunil's perspective, followed by a blank table for you.

Problem Statement	I am not getting time out of my business to spend with my family	
5 Whys	Question	Reason
1. Why?	Why am I not getting time out of my business to spend time with my family?	I am always stuck with many activities
2. Why?	Why am I always stuck with many activities?	I don't have capable managers and leaders to handle these activities
3. Why?	Why don't I have capable managers and leaders to handle these activities?	I have not recruited them
4. Why?	Why have I not recruited them?	I kept postponing the activity
5. Why?	Why did I keep postponing the activity?	**I don't trust anyone/I feel I can do it better [ROOT CAUSE]**

a. What should be my action to correct this problem?	I need to hire competent managers
b. By when should it be done?	31st October 2023
c. What are the steps to be followed to implement it	1. I will make a detailed analysis of the skills that is needed; 2. Shortlist the current employees who have the skills or hire 3 managers from outside; 3. Post the opportunities on LinkedIn and Naukri
d. Who will do it?	Ms. Meghana Nair (HR) + Myself

Now it's your turn! Every time you run into a roadblock, use this method to find clarity on the way ahead.

Problem Statement		
5 Whys	Question	Reason
1. Why?		
2. Why?		
3. Why?		
4. Why?		
5. Why?		

a. What should be my action to correct this problem?	
b. By when should it be done?	
c. What are the steps to be followed to implement it	
d. Who will do it?	

Footnote: The Five Whys technique was originally developed by the founder of Toyota Motor Corporation, Sakichi Toyoda. It was used within the company during the evolution of its manufacturing methodologies.

Note for Anne/Sunaina: Add QR code that leads to this video https://www.youtube.com/watch?v=P333Baxwtj4

NOTES: ✍

Reflection 2

Reaction Vs Reflection

After an equally stressful Friday and Saturday, Sunil was exhausted by the time he dropped into the cosy armchair at their favourite restaurant. They placed their orders and talked about their family, common friends, the weather…

Till Sunil asked, "How do you do it?"

"What do you mean? Be more specific," laughed Nitin.

"I mean how do you run a business and make it look so easy! Your company is doing great. And you haven't looked at your phone once since we got here an hour ago. In the meanwhile, I've had three calls and a ridiculous number of work-related messages for a weekend," said Sunil.

It got Nitin thinking of his typical day in the previous week.

08:00 AM

He usually returned home from an hour-long session with his personal trainer.

09:00 AM

He had breakfast with his wife and two daughters, who were almost identical in age to Sunil's children.

10:00 AM

He left for the office in his Porsche Panamera Turbo S that was the latest addition to the family. They had already done a couple of weekend road trips, and were planning a two-week long driving holiday during the upcoming school vacations.

12:00 PM

Nitin took his first work call of the day. A client was calling to appreciate his team for delivering a rush order and promised to place a bigger order. He walked around his minimalistic cabin as he spoke, happy to note that all his employees were in for the day.

04:00 PM

He had a short meeting with his chartered accountant, who brought up a few financial issues. But it was nothing that couldn't be fixed, since the company had a healthy cash flow. Over the years, he had successfully convinced both his clients and suppliers to deal with digital or online transactions in place of cash. This had increased his credibility.

05:00 PM

Nitin gave a lot of credit to his employees for the smooth running of the business. He had hired people with drive and ambition; they were always looking for ways to improve the company's earnings. He wrapped up after a staff meeting, addressing a few minor issues that came up, and planning his schedule for the next day.

06:30 PM

Tennis was one of Nitin's passions, and he played often. He was off to the court for a few games with fellow club members.

09:30 PM

A quiet dinner at home with the family.

10:00 PM

His usual bedtime, sometimes interrupted by a spontaneous movie or game night with his daughters. This was why he answered Sunil's text so late earlier that week.

Sunil felt a bit envious. "How do I also live like this," he asked. Nitin asked him in return: "What is the major cause of your stress when it comes to your business? I want you to really think deeply and answer."

Sunil said slowly, "I think it all boils down to cash flow. If I had proper cash flow management, I would be able to address a lot of the issues I'm facing."

"You're absolutely right," said Nitin. "For an entrepreneur, cash flow is like blood pressure. If it's too low, it can cause multiple issues. And if it is very high and not managed properly, it can be disastrous. Everything somehow circles back to the cash not being managed as effectively as it can be."

Sunil agreed that he had not taken time to think about the root of the problem. "Instead, I've been fighting these fires every day. Without fixing the actual issue, I'm not going to be able to solve anything."

"It's reflection versus reaction," explained Nitin. "Reaction is immediate and momentary, and it tends to be very strong. And at times, the reaction may be wrong, so you only get deeper in trouble." Plus, he added, these behaviours repeat themselves in other areas of our life, including personal finance. "My approach is to reflect. I say no to a lot of things because I put a lot of thought into it. But I do end up making more prudent decisions when it comes to money."

Nitin continued, "I believe that your thoughts define your actions. This scarcity mindset of not enough clients, not enough money is making you lose sight of the bigger picture. Ask yourself why your company and personal wealth has not been managed effectively enough, even though your business has been doing so well over the years."

This was exactly why Sunil had wanted to meet Nitin. There was no sugar-coating. He gave him the facts. But he did so with empathy. Which is what kicked in next.

Nitin gave him a tissue from the table and a pen and told him, "So, tell me. Why do people get into business?" Sunil said, "To make money, solve a problem they see, make a difference in the world around them, help the country, provide for their family…"

"Great! You've covered most of the common reasons. Now, from this list, if you had to choose, what would be your number one priority?"

Sunil didn't have to think too hard to answer. This was his list:

1. To provide for Saumya, Riya, Ishan
2. To provide for my employees/staff

Nitin asked, "Great! That's fair. But I'm curious to know why you chose that as your number one priority." Sunil replied, "No matter the bigger reasons, in the end, it all comes down to taking care of our own world. Saumya was my biggest support when I took over and had to grow the business. During the tough times, she and the kids encouraged me to keep going. As for my employees, some of them have been with me through thick and thin. They worked long nights and days to bring the company up - they showed a lot of ownership and dedication. I will always be grateful for that."

But Nitin was not done with this line of questions. He further asked, "Why is that the reason?" Sunil was mildly annoyed, but he expanded on his previous answer, saying, "I cannot imagine life without my wife and kids. They are the ones who give me purpose. I know I can depend on them for any support. Employees like Shankar, Avinash, and Meghana have been vital to the growth of the company. Their involvement means a lot to me personally, and we are bonded by the experiences we have been through."

The next question Sunil had to face was, "What are the consequences of not having your family and employees with you?" He had to think a while before he answered this. "Without them, I would not have any cash flow to run the business. Both family and employees are my motivators to earn and build up the company."

Nitin now asked, "Why would that worry you?" Sunil replied, "My family would not be living in the same level of comfort, my children would not be able to attend the best schools. My employees would not be with me to grow the company if I cannot pay them what they are worth."

It was time for the most important question of all: What are the steps you have taken to ensure that it doesn't happen?

Sunil admitted that Saumya was not involved in the business, and that he had not prepared for a scenario where he was not around. This made him feel a bit uncomfortable. If his absence resulted in zero cash flow, everything he worked for would come crashing down.

"As a first step, I'm going to sit with my chartered accountant to check and ensure a regular cash flow on a monthly basis. I'll look at where I can make changes and fixes so that this situation does not happen," he said.

Nitin had given Sunil something very important to reflect on. "I have forgotten what my primary motivating factor is. It's something I need to work on," he said.

Primary Motivating Factor Framework:

Second-generation entrepreneurs always have a reason for following in their family business. Every person has a different motivation. Sometimes, under the daily stresses and problems, it is easy to lose sight of that motivation. Here's a simple framework that can set you back on track.

Q1: Why do people start a business?

1. _______________________________________

2. _______________________________________

3. _______________________________________

4. _______________________________________

5. _______________________________________

Q2: From the above list, if YOU had to start a new business, what would be your #1 priority?

____

____

____

____

____

Q3: Why did you choose it as your #1 priority?

Q4: Why is that reason important to you?

Q5: What are the consequences of not having the opportunity to prioritise that reason?

Q6: Why would that worry you?

Q7: What are the steps you have taken to ensure that it doesn't happen?

____

____

____

____

Footnote: *The Primary Motivating Factor was described by Australian author and motivational speaker Allan Pease in his book 'Questions are the Answers: How to Get to 'Yes' in Network Marketing'.*

NOTES:

Reflection 3

The Wealth Blueprint

Nitin continued to reassure Sunil that all was not lost. "It happens at some point to every entrepreneur, Sunil. You are not alone. We just need to make sure your finances are in order," he said.

To help with the finances, Nitin pulled up a document on his phone.

"This is a wealth blueprint. Fill it in honestly, include your liabilities, and don't include the house you're staying at as an asset. It's not," he instructed Sunil. "Then there are the milestones. You already know a few: Ishan's college, Riya's education, a rough timeline of their weddings, when you'd like to retire… Figure out how much you need at each point and write it down."

Sunil said, "Homework! I can't remember the last time I had to do an assignment. But this might be the most important one I've done yet."

"I hope I was not too harsh. I just want to help in any way I can," said Nitin.

Sunil knew it was time to take some real action. "I absolutely appreciate the honesty, Nitin. I think I have been too busy with these minor things and forgotten what really matters. I will gladly take any help!"

Nitin said, "The first thing, of course, is to stop reacting immediately to every situation. Reflect on it calmly before making a decision. And next week, I'll connect you to a few people who can help you through the issues you're facing. One by one, we can tackle them all."

As they wrapped up dinner and parted ways, Sunil felt like he was waking up from a long sleep. He felt activated and energised, and was looking forward to boosting his business again. "Reflect, don't react," he repeated to himself as he drove home.

For the first time in a long time, he couldn't wait for Monday.

Task

My Wealth Blueprint: There are a few simple steps that you can take to get abundant wealth. One of those is getting your finances in order. Note down the following to identify your current net worth.

- List your assets (not including the property you live in)

- List your liabilities

- Subtract the total liabilities from the assets

My Networth in 10 years

Date after 10 years: _____________

Science Says 92 Percent of People Don't Achieve Their Goals. – INC.

And that's your net worth.

Assets	Amount (Rs)
Fixed Deposits	
Real Estate	
Stocks	
Mutual Funds	
Total Assets (A)	
Liabilities	
Total Liabilities (B)	
Net Worth (A-B)	

In addition, you need to prepare for the future. Some milestones may be children's education, weddings, your retirement. Writing it down makes it more real and easier to plan for.

My milestones	Year	Amount

Author's Note

Dear Reader, in the following pages, I share financial and investment rules that will guide your financial decisions. But if there's one thing you take away from this book, I hope it is this Wealth Blueprint. Need help? Email 1on1@naikwealth.in to book an appointment with me.

NOTES:

NOTES:

The Three Types of Income

Now that Sunil was done with his wealth blueprint, Nitin felt it was time to talk about types of income.

"How many types are there? I think I'm only focused on one: the active type," laughed Sunil.

Nitin agreed. "Having an active income is great, but you're only one person, and you're only human. You cannot be in more than one place at a time. So if you're looking at multiple channels of income, it has to be able to happen without you having to be there," he said.

That's where passive and portfolio incomes come into play.

There's a long list of passive income options: selling an ebook online, creating a course, selling stock photos, licencing your music, creating an app, network marketing, affiliate marketing, designing t-shirts, creating a monetised YouTube channel, Amazon affiliate marketing, blogging, creating a membership site, selling arts and crafts on Etsy, or even rental properties.

Sunil said, "I believe portfolio income would then include bank deposits, securities, peer-to-peer lending, high-yield savings account, annuities, investing in the stock market etc.."

"Exactly. In fact, if done well, your portfolio income can exceed your passive or even active income," said Nitin.

NOTES:

SECTION 2

Financial Rules

Introduction

Over the next few months, Sunil and Nitin had several conversations that ranged from investment decisions to business guidelines. Along the way, Nitin introduced Sunil to experts and mentors who advised him on the best practices to follow.

These learnings are condensed into two types of rules-financial/business and investment rules.

Rule 1

Pay Yourself First

Nitin had just asked Sunil if he took a salary from his business. Sunil said no, everything he needed was paid for directly from the company accounts.

"What would you say your role is in your company," asked Nitin.

"Hmmm… You could call me the CEO," said Sunil.

"If you hired a CEO who worked exactly how you are, how much would you have to pay him? That's what you should be paying yourself," explained Nitin.

This is a classic trap that many second-gen entrepreneurs fall into. They mistakenly think that the capital given by their parents or the capital from the business is free of cost. But it is not. They don't think of it as an investment. It has no value. And they don't look for ROI on that money since it is freely available.

Nitin continued, "The profit your company makes goes into three buckets: growth, reserves, and yourself. And there should be a balance between these. The business should not be starved for growth capital. At the same time, it should not have too much in terms of reserves. Because that means you are not putting enough into innovation and end up having a large amount of money on your balance sheet."

Sunil asked, "What is a good rule of thumb for splitting by percentage?"

Nitin suggested:

25% for growth capital

25% to reserves

45-50% for yourself/partners

PAY YOURSELF FIRST

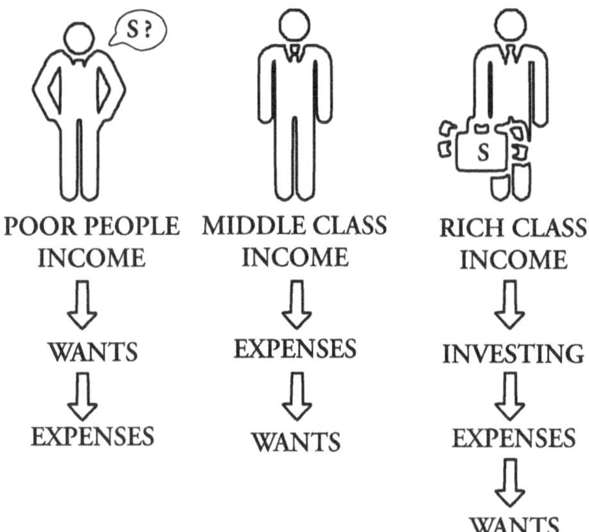

"You must be wondering why I'm placing such a premium on growth reserves," said Nitin.

"Sunil said, "I'm sure you have a good reason! Tell me, please."

Nitin recounted how he first came across the concept when his own company needed help.

At the end of the year, the finance guys would say that there is no money left for the founder. That's when Nitin started paying himself first.

Then, based on expert advice, they began setting aside money every month. The moment the money hit their account, it went into three buckets:

- For the founder

- For expenses

- For salary reserves

The last one was to be prepared in case of situations like Covid-19. The company wanted to build six months of reserves for salaries for all employees.

Further down the line, they added a bucket for future projects. Then one for a new branch in Delhi. Another for online initiatives. And so on.

This helped them fulfil all the company goals.

"Without these reserves, I would not be able to grow my company. It's something you should look into implementing soon," said Nitin.

NOTES: 🖎

Rule 2

50/30/20 Rule of Budgeting

"Once I start paying myself a salary, I suppose all my personal and family expenses will only have to be taken from this," said Sunil. Nitin said yes. "Take as much as you need as salary, but nothing more from the business. And follow the 50/30/20 rule of budgeting!"

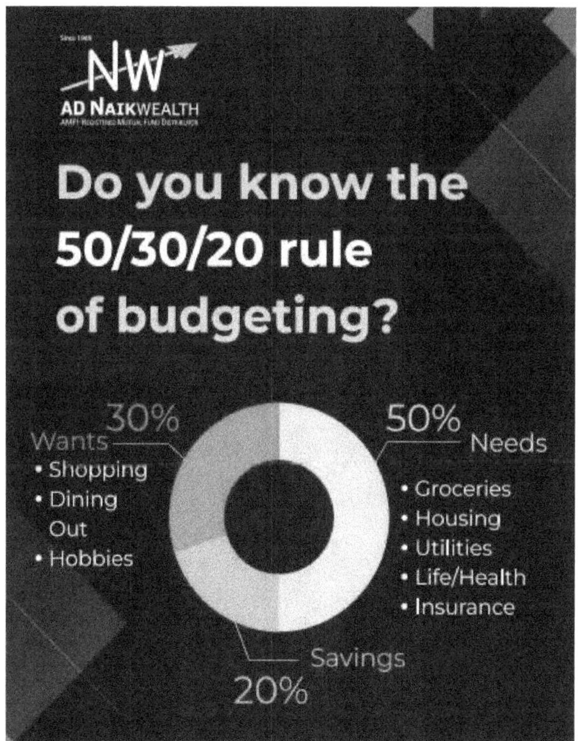

He explained that 50% of this income would go towards needs - groceries, house expenses, utilities, insurance etc. 30% goes into wants - everything from hobbies, shopping, eating out, as well as financial dreams like buying a new house, car, vacations, sending your kids to the best colleges abroad. And 20% is to save specifically for retirement.

While the recommended percentage to save is 20%, in India, the average number is closer to 30%. Entrepreneurs like Sunil should, as a thumb rule, save up to 40% and spend the rest on wants.

Sunil said with a laugh, "To be honest, I'm not sure what my expenses are. This will be a good way to find out!" The conversation then moved to how making money and savings have no connection. "The general feeling is that if I earn more, I'll end up saving more. But that doesn't happen. The expenses will automatically catch up," said Sunil.

Nitin agreed that saving is a habit, and you would end up spending more if that habit was not inculcated at an early stage. One of his mentors, Paresh, was a great inspiration for Nitin. "In his twenties, his first salary was Rs 4,000. His boss asked how much he was saving out of it. Paresh was surprised because it was such a small amount. How would he save anything? That's when he learned a valuable lesson: if you cannot save from a small amount, you will not be able to save even when you earn in lakhs."

This approach had helped Paresh build his wealth as his career grew over 20 years. "That's amazing! And I agree. If I earn Rs 15,000 a month and keep saying it's not enough and I don't save, it won't help when the salary increases to Rs 20,00,000 per month. The argument will remain the same because our lifestyle changes with income," said Sunil.

NOTES: ✍

Rule 3

Separate The Balance Sheets

Once Sunil began drawing a salary, there were now two separate balance sheets: business and personal. He was navigating the two with the help of Ananya, his new wealth manager. She had been recommended by Nitin. Like him, she was very straightforward.

The two balance sheets brought in fiscal prudence. Until then, Sunil had never paid too much attention to his personal expenses. Now, he knew where to pull back and where he was happy to indulge.

"We'll treat these two balance sheets as separate entities. The company has its own profits, and you have your income," said Ananya, pointing out that in the long run, it was safer for both parties.

For example, as long as it was simply school fees for the children, the company could manage at any time. But with Sunil's son Ishan entering college that year, the expenses would be very high. In case the company was not doing well when fees needed to be paid, Sunil could be certain that they could make the payments in time. "To put it simply, education cannot be dependent on the business cycle," said Ananya. The same principle applied for medical and other emergencies.

As for the business, knowing just how much money is available will help with future planning. This could be expansions, building a new office, renovating the factory, investing in new equipment... The possibilities are endless!

NOTES:

NOTES:

Rule 4

Parkinson's Law of Money

Nitin remembered a time when he realised that he had not set aside enough money for his children's education. He told his finance team that he wanted to save a certain amount per month. They said there was no cash flow to save. To do what Nitin wanted, they had to stop opening branches or cut people's salaries.

He gave another option. "Whatever money comes in each month, let's invest that in flexi deposits or liquid funds first." The team said this would mean that he would pay unnecessary taxes. Nitin agreed that if at the end of the year they were short on cash, he would pay it from the investments. In the meanwhile, they would keep only the bare minimum - only the amount that was needed for the week would remain accessible. The idea was that money out of sight can be saved, but money in sight always gets spent.

The calculated move paid off. He never had to dip into the investments.

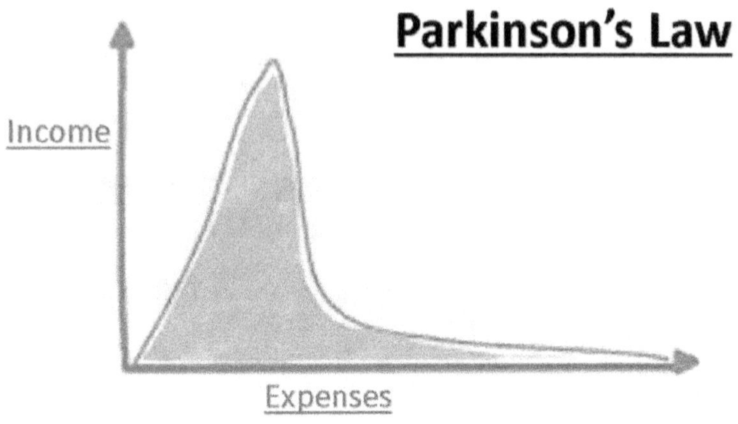

"That's Parkinson's Law in action," laughed Sunil, referring to a principle that says that cashflow adjusts for the amount of money available. "If you have more money in your account, your expenses will go up. The reverse is also true," he added. Nitin agreed, saying, "Business is a funny game. It will consume all the money you give, but also provide all the money you need. If you pay yourself more, it will generate enough profit to cover the cost."

Many times, these concepts are known, but are not always implemented. The key, they both agreed, is not to keep money in your bank account, not to keep excess money accessible to your finance department, not to keep money accessible to yourself also. And definitely be cautious with credit cards.

NOTES: 🖎

NOTES:

The Most Important Employee in Your Business

Much of Sunil's cash flow issues could have been avoided if the company accountants had been more vigilant. He shared this thought with Nitin, who said, "In the future, the focus should be on making our accountants think like a business owner or a Chief Financial Officer (CFO). They should not only look at ways to cut costs for the company, but also increase revenue."

Because a CFO is the CEO's right hand. They should be able to rely on the CFO's financial advice. And not make any decision without the CFO's input. As CEO of your own business, it's important to know your numbers, so that you can understand the financial impact of any decision you make.

Sunil agreed. "Money is one of the key employees in a business. They need to ensure that the money is working all the time," he said. They could recover money that was stuck. Or ask the important questions:

Where is the money?

Where is it getting spent?

What time is the money coming?

How much remains in the bank account?

NOTES:

Rule 6

Fix The Leaky Bucket:
A rupee saved is a rupee earned

Ananya, Sunil's wealth manager, had an important task. Do anything and everything that would restore cash flow to the business. They started with the low-hanging fruit: making sure creditors paid back their dues.

In Nitin's case, he wrote a letter to all new and existing clients, stating, "Henceforth, to serve you better, we would have a three-month grace period." He then appointed a person whose only duty was to follow up and collect his dues. Sunil implemented a similar policy, with quick results.

Ananya then introduced him to the concept of the "leaky bucket". They tackled four main areas.

1. Unnecessary and unused postpaid and landline bills that are auto-paid from the company accounts. These can be cancelled.

2. Insurance premiums. "One of our clients used to pay Rs 30,000 for a Rs 30 lakh premium. But now, there are plans that give a Rs 1 crore cover at the same price or less," said Ananya.

3. Overdrafts have unlimited tenure, and are like slow poison. And banks generally charge a higher rate of interest on overdraft. Fix this leak by converting overdrafts to term deposits instead.

4. Interest rates on loans. These can increase slowly and silently. "We advise people to move their home loans from higher to lower interest rates," said Ananya.

After all, a rupee saved is a rupee earned.

NOTES:

NOTES:

Rule 7

Stick To Your Core Activities

"What's your take on real estate development as a source for passive income," Sunil asked Nitin over coffee one evening.

"It depends on how you approach it," said Nitin. He recalled Gaurav, an acquaintance who owned a good deal of prime real estate in Mumbai. His friends encouraged him to construct something that would increase his income. He received multiple offers from builders and had several opportunities to become a real estate developer.

Much to everyone's surprise, he always refused. One day, Nitin asked Gaurav about the reasons for his refusal.

The response was very simple: "I have always been a business owner. I have never been a builder. That is not my core area of expertise or knowledge. I don't want to become a developer while running my current business."

Of course, there are multiple cases where people have gone on to become successful in industries outside their core domain. But Gaurav felt he would rather sell the land and exit because he had no experience or interest in becoming a builder. Nor did he want to leave his existing business. In his words, "I cannot ride two boats at the same time!"

The person who ended up buying these properties had the experience that Gaurav was cautious about. They wanted to construct residential properties, housing complexes, malls, and more. But it took 10 to 12 years just to get the basic permissions to start things off. And so it took them close to 15 years before they even recovered the money they put into the property.

Meanwhile, Gaurav created a decent passive income from the money he received while selling the land.

"What a great reminder that we should stick to what we know: when it comes to both business and investments," said Sunil.

NOTES:

NOTES:

Rule 8

Don't Lend, Gift

A couple is in bed at night, but the husband is worried and wide awake.

Wife: What is the matter?

Husband: I took a loan from my friend Ramesh, but I cannot repay it.

Wife: Be honest with him and tell him. I'm sure he will understand.

The next day, the husband goes to Ramesh and tells him he cannot repay the money. He comes back home and, that night sleeps deeply. However, from that day, Ramesh was not able to sleep well at all!

Nitin was sharing a joke he heard recently. Sunil laughed and said, "I couldn't agree more!"

Nitin added, "Yes, it's not advisable especially to lend to friends or family. Every time you see them spending without repaying you, it will make you jealous. It's a surefire way to lose both money and friendship."

Sunil agreed. His brother, Shekar, had lent money to his brother-in-law, Kedar. Kedar was not paying him back but was buying new cars and going on vacation. Shekar's father-in-law refused to get involved. So now relationships were sour between the whole family.

Nitin shook his head sadly at that. This is why his wife's grandfather had a mantra when it came to money: Give only what you can write off, both financially and emotionally.

"People came to him for loans to conduct their children's weddings. He would gently refuse to loan them a few lakhs, which they would repay over a few years. Instead, he would give them Rs 25,000 and say that they would not have to repay it," he explained.

"That's a good way of approaching such things. We can count on the older generation to pass on such wisdom," smiled Sunil.

NOTES: ✎

NOTES:

Investment Rules

Rule 1

Draw a Plan

"A pyramid is always built from the bottom up. It's a step-by-step process. That's the same way in which your wealth pyramid should be built."

~Ananya, Sunil's wealth manager

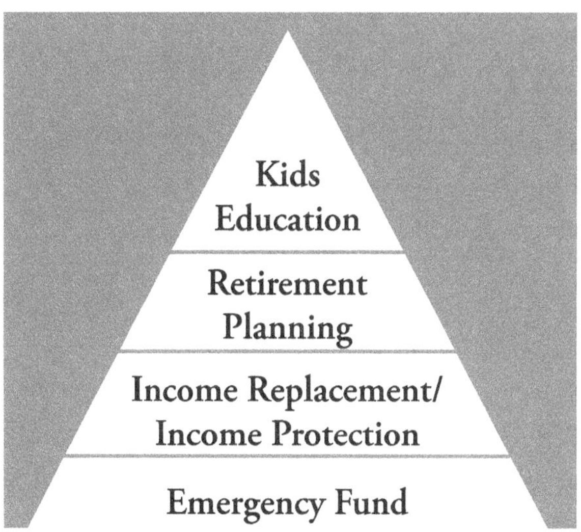

Even in creating and managing your own wealth, she explained, the very first step is to have an emergency plan in place. Then insurance, retirement, etcetera. "Investing has its own steps. You cannot directly jump to step number six, leaving behind the other steps and hoping everything will fall in place. It simply won't happen," said Ananya.

The numbers would look different for each person, based on their income and lifestyle. But to explain the concept, Ananya used some ballpark figures. Emergency fund should be six to nine months of expenses. To do this, one should know whether to invest in liquid funds or to invest in fixed deposits. Moving to retirement planning, Ananya said as a thumb rule, it should be about 30 times of your annual expense. Other expenses like kids education will depend on individual requirements.

When it comes to life insurance, Ananya suggested that he stick to a term cover. "What about medical insurance," asked Sunil.

Ananya said, "Before we get into that, can you tell me what kind of doctor and hospital you would prefer to go to in case you or your family are unwell?"

"The best doctors and the best hospital in the city, of course," replied Sunil.

Ananya continued, "Definitely. So, your medical insurance must cover the estimated costs of getting the best medical treatment. Find out how much your friends or relatives spent the last time they were admitted to the hospital. That will give you a rough idea of what you should be prepared for."

Sunil nodded in agreement. "That's a smart way of going about it," he said.

NOTES:

NOTES:

Rule 2

Stick To The Plan

Ananya had come up with a comprehensive wealth plan for Sunil. Once they went over the finer details, she said, "Sticking to this plan is equally important. Unless and until you implement it and you stick to it, it's not going to help you at all."

Sunil agreed that he would check in with her for any major decisions to see how it would affect their overall plan. To help with decision making and staying on track, Ananya told him two things to avoid.

Financial vultures: "Once you start accumulating more wealth, people are going to come to you and showcase products that look very good on paper. But they will not talk about the risk," she said. The projections look great on an Excel sheet. But there's usually nothing great in these financial products. This happens frequently with banks. Mis-selling has become rampant.

In fact, in December 2022, the Finance Minister of India had to issue a statement asking banks not to use unethical practices to sell insurance. Singer-actor Suchitra Krishnamoorthi also had a much-publicised case against an international bank for mis-selling financial products.

HSBC–Suchitra Krishnamoorthi case: The moral is do not mix insurance and investment

The moral of Krishnamoorthi's story is HNI or lesser mortal, the best way forward as far as investments by the laity are concerned is mutual fund, ideally open-ended.

Lending Money

It's okay to help a friend or a cousin in need, but never do it if it's going to put your budget in jeopardy. Even the most loyal ones are unable to pay back sometimes. In a situation like that. you'd be the one facing financial difficulties.

If you want to help someone, start by looking for other alternatives. Other ways in which you can contribute to the same situation. If that doesn't seem right. Loan a limited amount that can pass on as a gift and not debt. Think of a digit that won't shake your financial situation if not returned.

Toxic products: Sunil was reminded of someone who had been pursuing him like this. Sundar from Sunrise Developers would call almost every day. He wanted Sunil to invest in an upcoming project. Sunil felt that the potential returns looked great. Ananya disagreed. "If he's coming to you at 18% when the banks would ideally offer 14%, it's a red flag," she said. Grateful for this intervention, Sunil decided that he would turn down Sundar for good.

NOTES:

Rule 3

Don't Follow The Herd

*"Nitin, I heard that many of my
associates are investing in NFTs. I'm
thinking of doing the same."*

~Sunil

Nitin thought for a few seconds and then asked, "Can you put down a few other reasons why you should invest in this?" Sunil was not expecting this question. And he did not have any other concrete reason to do so.

It was a classic example of herd mentality. Over the years, people blindly invested in technology stocks which ended up being a tech bubble. Then in infrastructure. And the story went on even post-Covid. It was pharma and technology, and now, it is NFTs and cryptocurrency!

It's more comfortable to follow what others are doing. Even when things don't turn out the way you expect. As they say, misery loves company! Or in the words of American journalist James Surowiecki, "In conditions of uncertainty, humans, like other animals, herd together for protection."

75

However, it does not work that way with investing.

"You may feel that you will make a good amount of wealth over a period of time, but it's not always the case," explained Nitin. He gave the example of Bollywood actor Arshad Warsi, who didn't have any knowledge of stocks, but invested in certain companies because many others did. He ended up losing a lot of hard-earned money.

Please do not believe everything you read in the news. Maria and my knowledge about stocks is zero, took advice and invested in Sharda, and like many other, lost all our hard earned money.

4:07 PM · Mar 2, 2023 · **1.7M** Views

NOTES: ✍

NOTES:

Rule 4

Protect Yourself

Ananya believed that Sunil was ready to move on to the next stage of wealth management and financial planning: protecting his business, and his family. It was time to buy a keyman insurance.

"Your wife is a director of the company, and in due time, you'll add your children to the board as well. But you are the one running this company for the past 20+ years. So, God forbid, something were to happen to you, what happens to the business," asked Ananya.

Sunil said, "There will still be contracts to fulfil, salaries to pay, bills and expenses to take care of… If we close the business without any notice, my employees would be out of a job. They will need to find new jobs. But that will not happen overnight, so they will suffer."

Ananya said, "This is where keyman insurance comes in. It is a policy that will take care of, let's say, one year's expenses. Whoever steps into your place has that time to decide what to do with the business. Will they sell it? Will someone take over and run it? Will they merge with another company? They will have time to choose without making a rushed decision. This helps with succession in case any tragedy strikes before you have made plans."

She introduced Sunil to the ART of insurance planning: a simple three-step process that would keep his mind at ease, while protecting all aspects of his life.

NOTES:

NOTES: ✍

Rule 5

Quick Money Or More Money

"How long is a long-term investment for you," asked Ananya, the wealth manager. Sunil said, "How about six months?" They laughed and agreed that it was a ridiculous expectation. Investments are like planting a seed. You need to water it, nourish the soil, protect the plant as it starts growing and hope that it grows into a tree that bears fruit.

Ananya put forth a scenario to Sunil.

"Let's say your friend needs money, and he says he will return it in three days. He is very honest and dependable, and you'll definitely get it back. What will your answer be?"

"Probably yes," said Sunil.

"Now, how much interest will you charge?"

"Probably none."

"Now, imagine he says he needs it for six months. Will you charge him interest then?"

"Again, probably not."

"But if he says he needs it for three years, because he's buying a house, you will probably reach some sort of agreement on interest."

"Maybe not at the market rate, but something that will benefit me."

"Another scenario: he asks you for money for five to eight years since he is starting a restaurant."

"I'll probably give him a business loan with lesser interest or reach some sort of profit-sharing agreement."

"And what if he says that he's starting a luxury hotel in Goa? It's got a prime location in a tourist-heavy spot. You might not see returns for a long time, but when they come, they will be extremely good."

"I'd love to be a partner in such a venture! The more stake I hold, the more I will profit."

Ananya approved of this answer, and gave another example. 28 years ago, some people believed in the potential of HDFC Bank and invested in them as shareholders. Since they had money to invest long term, this was a good decision to make. HDFC Bank is now one of the largest players in the financial world. "When the timelines are longer, it is always good to be a part owner. Today, they are reaping the benefits. But if you need your money back in one to three years, it is better to lend," she said.

The growth of any business is never linear, it will be volatile, going up and down like a heartbeat. Ananya continued, "You have to make these long term versus short term investments based on your financial goals and the availability of your money. In the long term, the graph tends to always move upward."

The lessons here are:

- Shorter the term, lend. But expect savings bank returns.

- Medium term, expect bank fixed deposit returns.

- Longer term, this is money you should invest. Become a partner in the company's growth story.

"But we do the complete opposite. We invest short term in stock markets and expect to get profits in a few days. Long term, we put our money in fixed deposits," said Ananya. She expanded on how the bank is basically a money lender at the end of the day. They lend your parked money to other business owners at higher interest rates. For instance, they might lend at 11% and give us 7% on our deposit. The business to which they are lending would have made 18-25%.

So, why let your money lie idle? Put it to work and get higher returns in the long term.

Rule 12: Leveraging and timing the market <Need to finalize the name of this rule>

Leveraging is all about timing the market and trying to get it right.

<Need additional explanation for this + the source/story of the man in Hyderabad who put a plaque outside his house saying it was built because he invested in Reliance>

The same can be said of leveraging assets. Sunil remembered a story about an acquaintance who bought real estate and made good returns on it. So, he sold that property and bought two more. He made more money, sold these two and bought three more.

This time, he started taking loans on the properties. Fast forward to today, where he owned real estate worth Rs 45 crore, but all mortgaged to the banks. None of the properties are sellable, because they were valued at a higher right while they were pledged. He would not be able to repay the whole loan.

Thus, proving the words of American billionaire and vice chairman of Berkshire Hathaway, Charlie Munger, "There are only three ways a smart person can go broke: liquor, ladies and leverage."

NOTES:

NOTES:

Rule 6

Be an investor, not a collector

"A portfolio should be there for a reason - not because you think it's a candidate for the world's best investment." Carl Richards, Author and Financial Planner

The latest IPO. The NASDAQ Next 20. The newest cryptocurrency. A revamped company. Top 10 mutual funds. The best-performing stocks.

You read all about it. And you want to buy all of it.

But don't eat the next Apple or drink the next Coca-Cola.

Make your investments wisely. Put thought into it.

And as I always say, when in doubt, write a full page on why you must and should invest in a particular stock.

NOTES:

NOTES: ✍

Rule 7

Core and Satellite Portfolios

There are two types of portfolios: core and satellite

Core portfolios are required to help you achieve your life goals. It could be anything, buying a house, retirement planning, buying a new car, going out for vacations, children, education, marriage, all those things.

A satellite portfolio is not mapped to any of your goals. It is just for you to explore and experiment.

An international client asked why we would not invest in international funds for her. Her basic goals can be met in her current portfolio. Investing into a particular stock or market needs a lot of in-depth analysis. Neither she nor I could keep an eye on what's happening in the US market.

The time had not yet come to invest in US stocks simply because she had not yet completed her bucket of basic needs as an investor. Something like this would be part of a satellite portfolio.

As a rule of thumb, 80% should be in your core portfolio. The remaining 20% is satellite. This is a good benchmark, to begin with. You can then move it to 60/40.

ASSET CLASS / COMPONENT	LIQUIDITY	VOLATILITY	YIELD
PROPERTY	HIGHLY ILLIQUID	KNOWN TO BE GIVING A STABLE RETURN	DEPENDENT THE MARKET
EQUITY	GENERALLY LIQUID	KNOWN TO BE HIGHER RISK	KNWON TO HAVE HIGHER RETURN
BONDS	LIQUIDITY IS DEPENDENT ON MARKET DEMAND	DEPENDENT ON THE MARKET	KNOWN TO BE GIVING A STABLE RETURN
COMMODITIES	LIQUIDITY IS DEPENDENT ON MARKET DEMAND	KNOWN TO BE HIGHER RISK	KNWON TO HAVE HIGHER RETURN
CASH	LIQUID	-	-

Once you are done with all your investments, you could look at alternative investments. Don't make the common mistake of jumping to the alternatives before you do your basic investing.

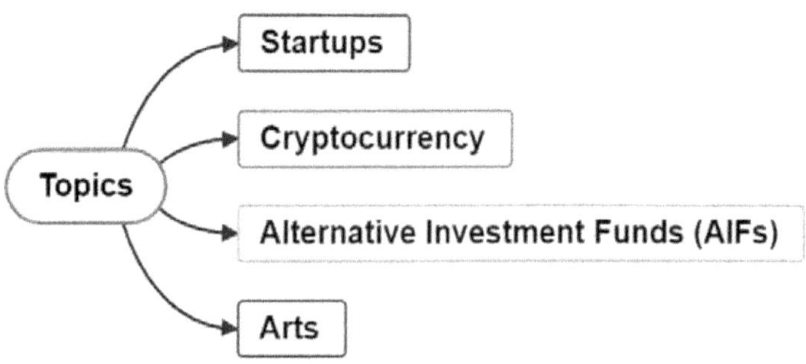

NOTES:

NOTES:

9 Lies of Wealth Creation

9 Lies of Wealth Creation

In the last few pages, we have seen Sunil's journey to effective wealth management. These rules will guide you as you take the same journey.

But before you begin, a few things to be aware of. There are many misconceptions about managing your money and making it work. What can you believe? What shouldn't you fall for? How can you keep your finances safe? Find out in this section:

The Seven Lies of Wealth Creation.

Lie 1

Income is Equal to Wealth

People think that they need to earn a lot of money, and that their business should be making a lot of profit before they start saving. But this is not true.

When you start your business, you cannot save because you need to pay back your loans, or you're using the income to expand. Later, costs go up, so you are not able to save.

But savings has nothing to do with your income or the situations you face.

It is purely a state of mind. Take for example American philanthropist Ronald Read. He was a janitor in a school and petrol station attendant. But when he died in 2014, he was worth over $8 million. According to Wikipedia, he "had achieved this by investing in dividend-producing stocks, avoiding the stocks of companies he did not understand such as technology companies, living frugally, and being a buy and hold investor in a diversified portfolio of stocks with a heavy concentration in blue chip companies".

It is possible even today. Let's see a real life example. We've seen Hemanth* with an annual income of Rs.12 lakh, consistently invested since 2003. He invested a total amount of Rs.1.26 crore. The current value of this investment is Rs. 2.81 crore.

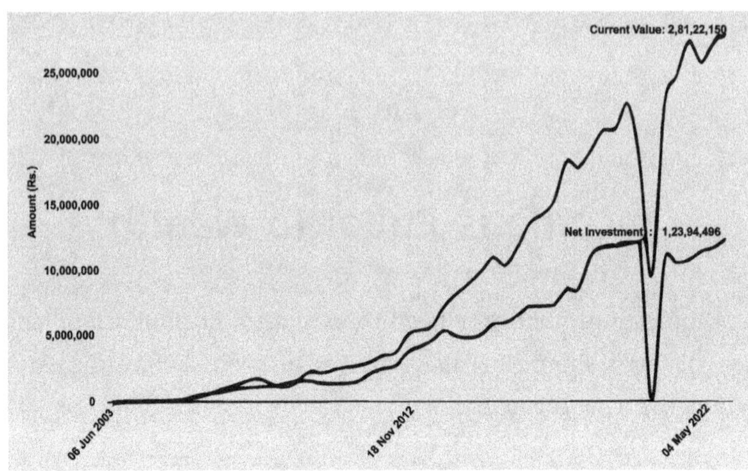

Growth of Hemanth's investments over the years

At the same time, Bharath, a brand manager for a large media company with Rs 48 lakh annual income has not been able to see this growth. He invested only Rs 37 lakh, and has a current value of Rs 76 lakh.

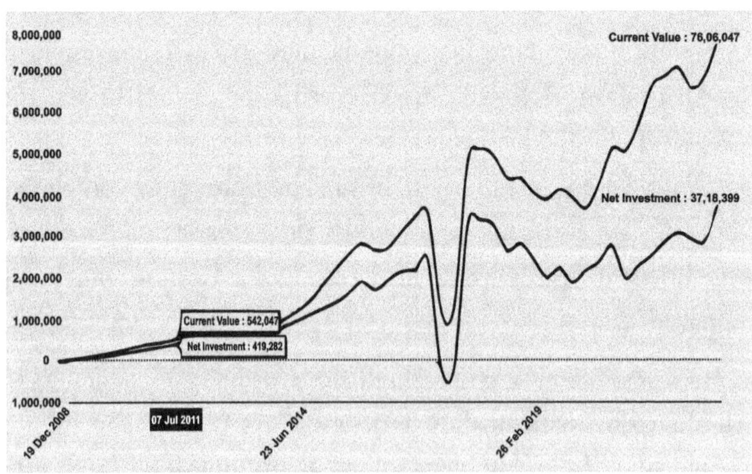

Growth of Bharath's investments over the years

In both cases, there have been ups and downs in the graph. But over the years, it always trends upwards. That's why we say that this has nothing to do with income.

Savings has to do with the mindset and the belief system.

When the belief is that you need a lot of money in income or profits to create wealth, that will never happen. As a thumb rule, you should start saving at least 30% of your profits and increase it with time.

If you are not able to save today, you'll never be able to save tomorrow.

NOTES:

Lie 2

Returns are Equal to Wealth

Warren Buffett is one of the richest people in the world, with a net worth of \$104 billion. But in the book *The Psychology of Money*, we learn of his admiration for mathematician Jim Simons.

Simons was a mathematics professor at Stony Brook University and later, founded the Renaissance Technologies hedge fund. Medallion, the main fund, has earned over \$100 billion in trading profits since it was started in 1988. Simons himself has a net worth of \$25.5 billion. Today, he has become synonymous with the idea of using mathematical models and algorithms to trade in financial markets.

So, why exactly is Buffett impressed with Simons? Because this whole idea of using mathematical models and algorithms to trade in financial markets has given 66% returns year on year. Which is outstanding!

The difference between their amount of wealth is only because of compounding. Buffett's fund, Berkshire Hathaway, might comparatively have a lower rate of returns at 22%. But his money has been at work for more years - since 1965 - which explains the massive gap between their net worths.

Which is why we say that the creator of wealth is not returns. It is compounding year on year on year on year....

To be successful in the market, you have to survive in the market. If you survive, you will definitely create a lot of wealth. There's a simple formula for this.

$$\text{Amount} = P\left(1 + \frac{r}{100}\right)^n$$

Where

P = Principal

r = Rate of interest

n = Number of years

Everyone tends to focus on 'r', but the most important is 'n'. That's where the magic happens, with compounding.

After all, in the words of the famous Albert Einstein, "Compound interest is the eighth wonder of the world. He who understands it, earns it. He who doesn't, pays it."

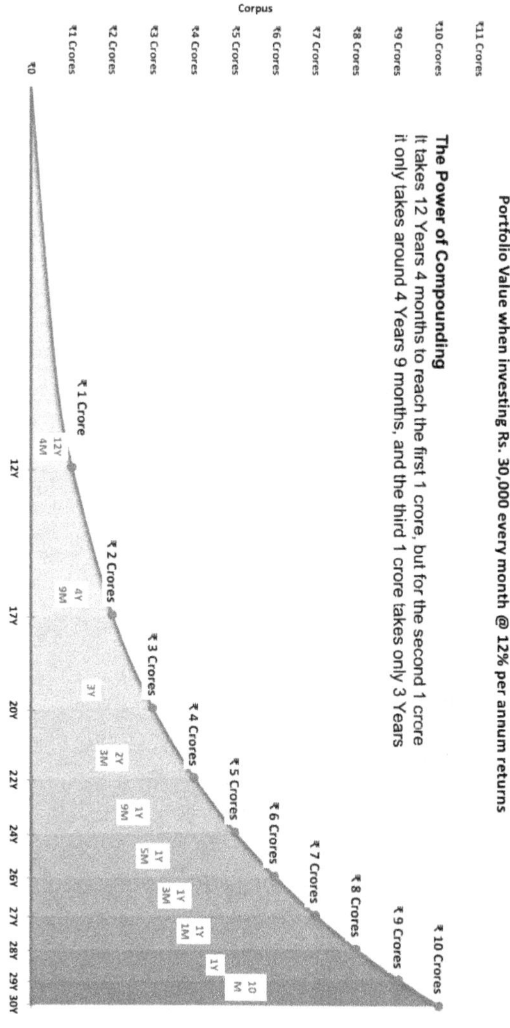

NOTES:

Lie 3

Knowledge is Equal to Wealth

*"If you don't read the newspapers,
you are uninformed. If you do read
them, you are misinformed."*

~Mark Twain, American author

With so much data available online, there is a high chance of going to the wrong source for knowledge.

How to build a STRONG crypto portfolio?
@Akshat Shrivastava | Vauld

Vauld · 4.3K views · 1 month ago

 CRYPTO PORTFOLIO | Watch...   8 key moments

Vauld - Invest in Style || Crypto is Future || Start AIP in Vauld || Booming Bulls

Booming Bulls · 34K views · 8 months ago

I INVESTED IN A FIXED DEPOSIT!

warikoo · 2.2 lakh views · 8 months ago

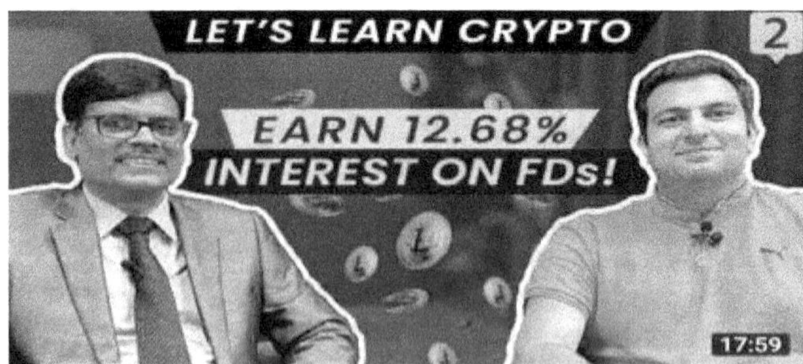

Buy & Sell CRYPTOS Easily & Earn 12.7% INTEREST on FDs | Basics of Cryptocurrency...

P R Sundar · 1.8 lakh views · 9 months ago

Take for instance the story of Vauld, a crypto exchange that was promoted widely by 'finance influencers'. The company eventually stopped paying its creditors and filed for bankruptcy. Those who had followed the advice of these influencers ended up losing their investments. They also learnt a lesson the hard way - know who to trust with your money.

When the source is incorrect, the results will not be great either! Getting knowledge from those whose main work is creating content? It is often misleading, or packaged to make it go viral. How much knowledge can you absorb in 15 to 30 seconds, while being distracted by many other notifications?

Then there are those who try to show off their knowledge by misrepresenting their earnings. This Twitter thread is a great example. One user posts about her earnings from Tata Steel stock and claims to be sitting with a Rs 2.1 crore profit. In response, another user does the math and proves that her numbers are impossible.

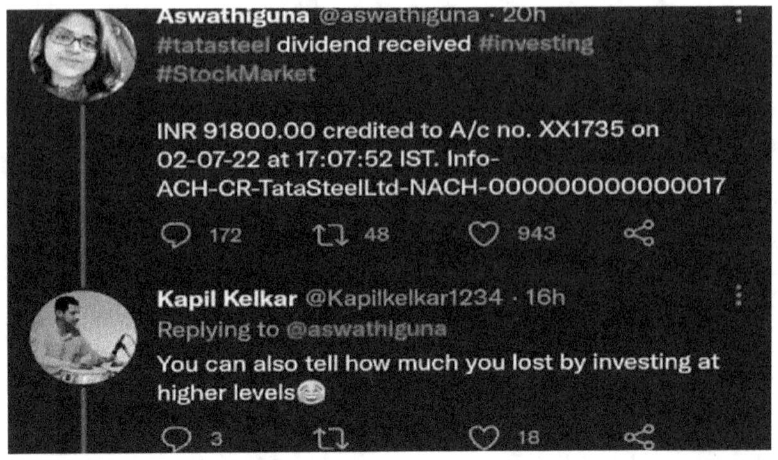

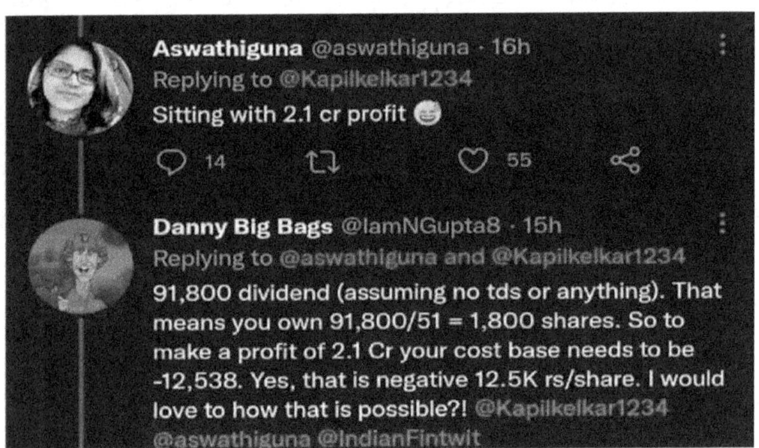

Just remember, there are no free lunches in life. Somewhere down the line, you will pay for it.

As the saying goes, "Half-baked knowledge is a dangerous thing." Ensure that you know what you are doing. Or for the best results, do your research and work with experts who know how to make your money grow!

Know the credibility of your sources before following their advice. For instance, books will give you serious knowledge. A lot of thought and time goes into them, and they are created with the intention of sharing the writer's expertise. Here are three classics that will help you on this journey of wealth creation.

NOTES:

Lie 4

Intelligence is Equal to Wealth

"With enough insider information and a million dollars, you can go broke in a year."
~Warren Buffet, American investor

Let me share a story of a very intelligent man. A man whose IQ was between 190 to 200. Keep in mind that most people have an IQ of 85 to 115. This man is none other than Sir Isaac Newton, a 17th-century English mathematician, physicist, astronomer, alchemist, theologian, and author who was described in his time as a natural philosopher. He was a key figure in the Scientific Revolution and the Enlightenment that followed.

However, even he had challenges while investing in the stock market. Here's his story. He was an early investor in the South Sea Company, which was a scheme for managing British government debt. Despite early profits, the stock was volatile. Although Newton first liquidated his stake at a huge profit, he kept jumping back in as the bubble kept growing.

His biggest mistake was investing almost at the peak, exactly when the bubble burst. Newton allegedly said that he could "calculate the motions of the heavenly bodies, but not the madness of people".

Being intelligent is not enough when it comes to investing. It is also important to be prudent. Focus on your own behaviour, not on the market's behaviour.

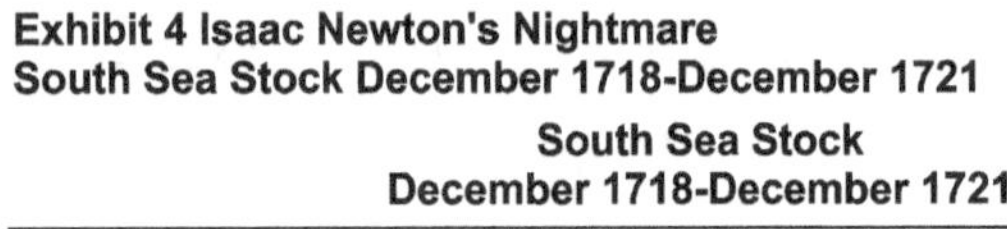

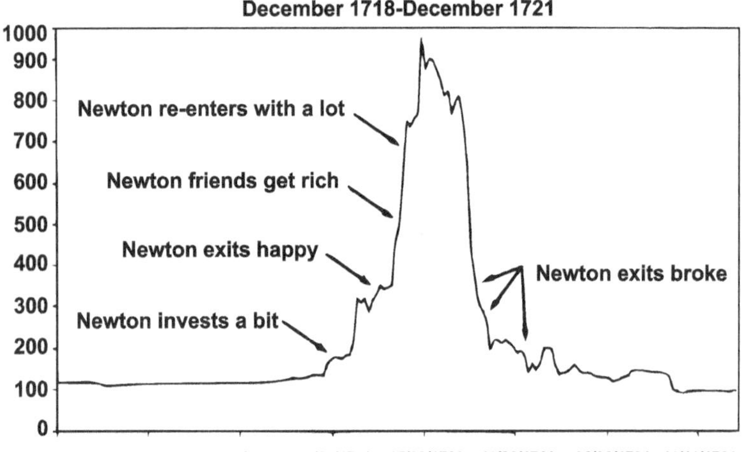

Marc Faber, Editor and Publisher of "The Gloom, Boom & Doom Report."

Newton owned £22,000 (nearly £4 million in 2023) of South Sea stock. Estimates say that he lost up to £20,000 (equivalent to £3.68 million in 2023). The above graph shows where he entered, the growing value, when the bubble burst, and how much he left with.

Another brilliant example is American author Mark Twain, who wrote popular novels such as Tom Sawyer and The Adventures of Huckleberry Finn. Despite his intelligence, he was really bad at investing!

According to Time magazine, "He lost money on an engraving process, on a magnetic telegraph, on a steam pulley, on the Fredonia Watch Company, on railroad stocks. He once turned down a chance to buy into Bell Telephone even though he had one of the nation's first residential phones."

Mark Twain's financial investments are a cautionary tale on risk-taking that all investors should heed

LARRY MACDONALD
SPECIAL TO THE GLOBE AND MAIL

Mark Twain: Investment Lessons from a Literary Legend

Rod Tyler, CFP, R.F.P., CLU
Financial Advisor at The Tyler Group

13 articles   + Follow

The 19ᵗʰ Century Start Ups That Cost Mark Twain His Fortune.

The Paige Compositor. Mark Twain lost almost all his money after investing in this.

Twain's saga of investments is still a popular cautionary tale in newspapers, blogs and social media! His biggest blunder was perhaps investing in a typesetter machine. When he saw that it worked faster than its rivals, he sunk all his money into it. The only issue was that it did not work consistently! He faced similar problems when he decided to start up his own publishing house.

Despite being a smart man, he loved taking risks. He seemed to have learnt his lesson many decades later when he wrote, "There are two times in a man's life when he should not speculate: when he can't afford it and when he can."

NOTES:

NOTES:

Lie 5

Money is Equal to Wealth

Sushil Kumar, who won Rs. 5 crore in Kaun Banega Crorepati in 2011, describes it as being the "worst phase" of his life. Post taxes, this would have netted him about Rs. 3.5 crore. If invested properly, he could have doubled it. He would have been set for life.

Instead, he lost all his money by lending to friends for different ventures that failed. In a Facebook note he wrote in 2020, he said that he'd be asked to attend events 15 days in a month after his win. He began investing in a few businesses just to have something to say to the journalists who interviewed him.

Mantu Kumar Sushil
22 h · 🌐

केबीसी जितने के बाद का मेरे जीवन का सबसे बुरा समय

2015-2016 मेरे जीवन का सबसे चुनौती पूर्ण समय था कुछ बुझाइए नही रह था क्या करें।

लोकल सेलेब्रिटी होने के कारण महीने में दस से पंद्रह दिन बिहार में कहीं न कहीं कार्यक्रम लगा ही रहता था।इसलिए पढ़ाई लिखाई धीरे धीरे दूर जाती रही।

उसके साथ उस समय मीडिया को लेकर मैं बहुत ज्यादा सीरियस रहा करता था और मीडिया भी कुछ कुछ दिन पर पूछ देती थी कि आप क्या कर रहे हैं इसको लेकर मैं बिना अनुभव के कभी ये बिज़नेस कभी वो करता था ताकि मैं मीडिया में बता सकूं की मैं बेकार नही हूँ ।
जिसका परिणाम ये होता था कि वो बिज़नेस कुछ दिन बाद डूब जाता था।

इसके साथ केबीसी के बाद मैं दानवीर बन गया था और गुप्त दान का चस्का लग गया था महीने में लगभग 50 हज़ार से ज्यादा ऐसे ही कार्यों में चला जाता था ।

इस कारण कुछ चालू टाइप के लोग भी जुड़ गए थे और हम गाहे-बगाहे खूब ठगा भी जाते थे जो दान करने के बहुत दिन बाद पता चलता था।

पत्नी के साथ भी सम्बन्ध धीरे धीरे खराब होते जा रहे थे
वो अक्सर कहा करती थी कि आपको सही गलत लोगों की पहचान नही है और भविष्य की कोई चिंता नही है,ये सब बात सुनकर हमको लगता था कि हमको नही समझ पा रही है इस बात पर खूब झड़गा हो जाया करता था ।

हालांकि इसके साथ कुछ अच्छी चीजें भी हो रही थी दिल्ली में मैंने कुछ कार ले कर अपने एक मित्र के साथ चलवाने लगा था जिसके कारण मुझे लगभग हर महीने कुछ दिनों दिल्ली आना पड़ता था इसी क्रम में मेरा परिचय कुछ जामिया मिलिया में मीडिया की पढ़ाई कर रहे लड़कों से हुआ फिर आईआईएमसी में पढ़ाई कर रहे लड़के फिर उनके सीनियर,फिर जेएनयू में रिसर्च कर रहे लड़के,कुछ थियेटर आर्टिस्ट आदि से परिचय हुआ जब ये लोग किसी विषय पर बात करते थे तो लगता था कि अरे!मैं तो कुएँ का मेढ़क हूँ मैं तो बहुत चीजों के बारे में कुछ नही जानता।

Without proper financial planning, even a bonanza like this cannot last. This ties in to the lies that knowledge and intelligence are equal to wealth. He had enough intelligence to win the top prize in one of the toughest game shows. But when it came to money, he did not have the financial literacy to make good investments.

In India, especially, there is no focus on financial education at a school level. What we learn is often from our parents, who came from a different era. What worked for Sunil's father in business would not necessarily work for him in today's digital world. There are a lot more checkpoints, and each entrepreneur needs to build credibility in different ways. Second gen entrepreneurs like Sunil often have a lot of unlearning to do.

NOTES: ✍

Lie 6

Prediction is Equal to Wealth

*"Those who have knowledge, don't predict.
Those who predict, don't have knowledge."*

~Lao Tzu, Chinese Philosopher

People love predictions. They always have. The above quote is close to 2,000 years old! However, it is ridiculous to follow predictions.

A simple Google search will show you that two different research houses predict two different things for the same company in the same time period. How do we know who is right? Then there is a third research house predicting something entirely different. Finally, none of what they say may come true!

Citi Warns Oil May Collapse to $65 by the Year-End on Recession

Serene Cheong

Published On 12:03 PM IST, 05 Jul 2022
Last Updated On 12:21 PM IST, 05 Jul 2022

☐ Save

(Bloomberg) -- Crude oil could collapse to $65 a barrel by the end of this year and slump to $45 by end-2023 if a demand-crippling recession hits, Citigroup Inc. has warned.

That outlook is based on an absence of any intervention by OPEC+ producers and a decline in oil investments, analysts including Francesco Martoccia and Ed Morse said in a report. Brent, the global crude benchmark, last traded near $113 a barrel.

JPMorgan Sees 'Stratospheric' $380 Oil On Worst-Case Russian Cut

Joe Carroll

Published On 10:43 AM IST, 02 Jul 2022
Last Updated On 10:44 AM IST, 02 Jul 2022

☐ Save

(Bloomberg) -- Global oil prices could reach a "stratospheric" $380 a barrel if US and European penalties prompt Russia to inflict retaliatory crude-output cuts, JPMorgan Chase & Co. analysts warned.

Predictions are only as good as crystal ball gazing. How many predicted Covid-19? Or that Russia would invade Ukraine? Just refer to this researcher's article in Al Jazeera which categorically said that it would not happen!

No, Russia will not invade Ukraine

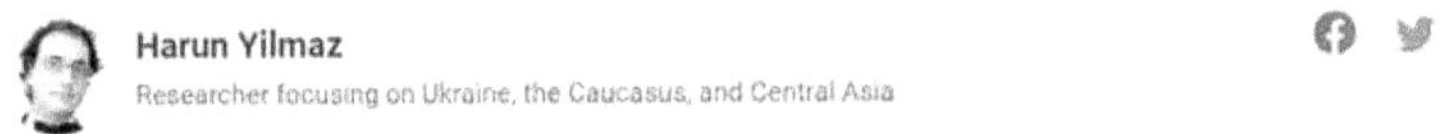

Harun Yilmaz
Researcher focusing on Ukraine, the Caucasus, and Central Asia

The proof is in the numbers. An analysis was done of 6,582 public market calls made by 68 financial experts between 2005-2012. Their average accuracy rate was less than half-47%.

No one can predict which way the market will go so don"t fall prey to "sure shots" or "insider information". You will have higher possibilities of making money if you do your own research!

NOTES:

NOTES:

Lie 7

Timing is Equal to Wealth

What happens today is that some stockbrokers are out there, giving you tips on when to buy, which stock to buy, what time to buy, when to exit. They're trying to make quick money and fast money. And will try to influence you to do the same.

This is what timing the market is focused on. You end up in a cycle of buy, sell, buy, sell, buy, sell, sell, buy... And many times you will end up losing (refer to Newton's example earlier in the book).

Additionally, the Securities and Exchange Board of India (SEBI) has shared information that shows that out of 4.5 Mn individual traders in futures and options (FY22), only 11% made a profit. The constant entering and exiting is clearly not giving returns.

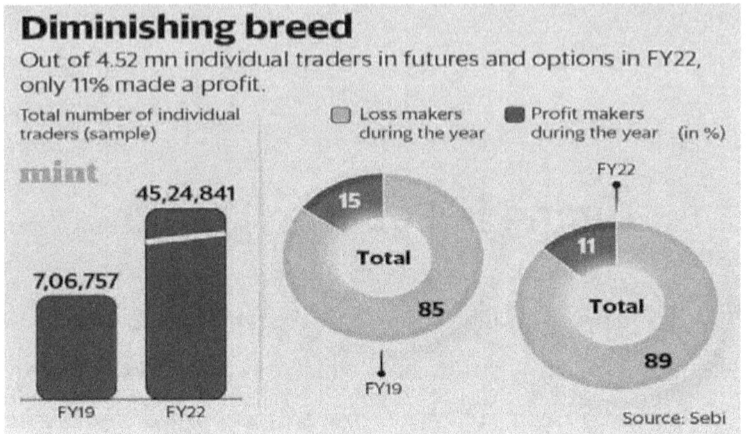

Compare this to someone who just invested and stayed, going with the flow. In the long run, such investments give great returns. We have the real-life example of Warren Buffett. He started at the age of 11, with $5,000. By the time he was 30, he made his first million. In his mid-50s, he turned into a billionaire. And past 60 is when he made 90% of his wealth.

NOTES:

NOTES:

Lie 8

What's popular is
not equal to wealth

Bored Ape floor drops below $100K as
NFT market takes a huge hit

Visit

The NFT craze convinced people to give up day jobs to trade pictures of apes. Today, the graph has crashed.

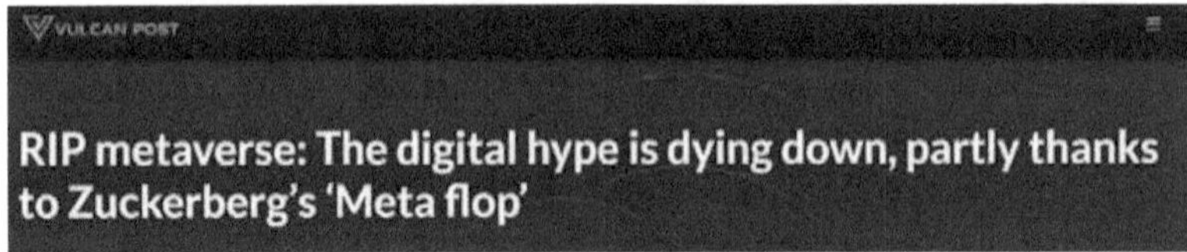

TECH FACEBOOK

Mark Zuckerberg takes the blame for failing to spot the post-pandemic downturn as he slashes 11,000 staff from Meta's headcount

Mark Zuckerberg, the founder of Facebook, sunk millions into the metaverse - he even renamed his company because he believed it was the future. After thousands have been laid off due to this bad investment, the company is slowly moving away from the metaverse.

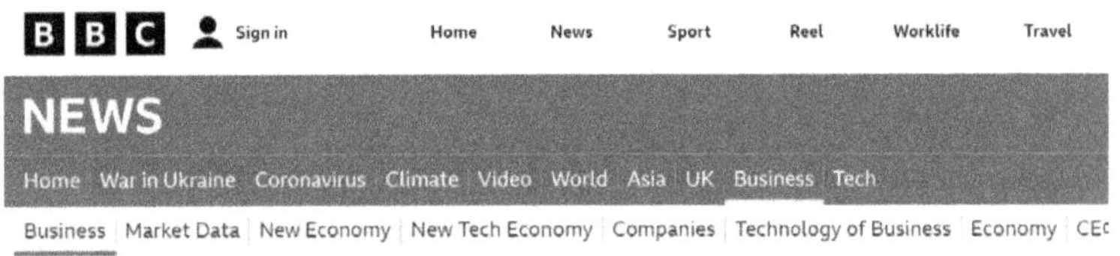

Was Tulip Mania really the first great financial bubble?

This rush to invest in the most fancy, new or popular thing is not new. The 17th century saw a tulip mania. In Holland, traders believed that tulip bulbs were going to be worth millions.

This was a bubble that burst in due time because everyone became a tulip bulb trader overnight.

The lesson here is to stay away from these popular things if you want to keep your money safe. If everyone's buying real estate, avoid it. This happened in 2013 during the peak of the real estate boom. Everyone owned two houses. It left us wondering, "If everyone is an owner, who is the buyer?" Over the last decade, it has been a no-return period for real estate. A lot of builders went behind bars, and the government came down heavily on the sector. RERA regulations were intensified.

In 2020, during the Covid-19 pandemic, even a techie became a trader and stock market expert. They became advisors and started telling people what to buy, and what not to buy. So 2021 became a time to be careful with your equity.

Look out for feelers when you are in a group of people. If all of them are talking and hyping up a particular stock, stay away from it. This is how the madness builds. It is human nature. The key is to be cautious when everyone is greedy.

When a popular investment opportunity is given to you, sleep over it. It's extremely important to reflect on why so many people are investing in it and why you should do it too. See if you can write a whole page as to why you choose to invest. Give yourself concrete reasons to do so.

NOTES: ✍

<h1 style="text-align:center">Lie 9</h1>

Real estate is equal to wealth

Indians love to invest in three things:

1. Real Estate

2. Fixed Deposits

3. Gold

There is a common misconception that property is a good way to hold cash.

But it is NOT cash. It is not guaranteed that you will find the right tenant. Or that the income will be equal to the taxes that must be paid on time. Not to mention the regular maintenance required on properties.

Let's take the case of Nariman Point, a prime commercial address in the heart of Mumbai. You have the big banks, law firms, and chartered accountants. When you give an address there, it has a wow factor.

One particular gentleman, a business owner, invested a lot in real estate in this area. With time, the cost of real estate in that part of Mumbai skyrocketed. Most people and businesses started moving to the suburbs. Many commercial properties also came up there to meet the demand for space.

The business owner did not get the kind of appreciation in the capital that he was expecting. Though he has real estate, he does not have liquidity. People do not have or do not want to spend so much to rent or buy. They also realise that employees are in the suburbs and will spend too much time commuting, which is another issue. For business houses, that becomes an added advantage that we are taking care of the employees by having a space close to where they live.

The problem with real estate is that it is not an asset that always goes up. It will have its own days of volatility, and it's illiquid as an asset. In this case, people end up selling it for far lower than they purchased. There are no gains.

AN ILLIQUID ASSET IN RETIREMENT BECOMES A LIABILITY!

For owners to repair or recreate the buildings, it takes huge capital. When you invest in real estate, there are always additional expenses: repairs, maintenance, etc. The return is only 4% - it does not appreciate for years. People do not realise this.

The same can be said of leveraging assets. One businessman bought real estate and made good returns on it. So, he sold that property and bought two more. He made more money, sold these two and bought three more.

This time, he started taking loans on the properties. Fast forward to today, where he owned real estate worth Rs 45 crore, but all mortgaged to the banks. None of the properties are sellable because they were valued at a higher right while they were pledged. He would not be able to repay the whole loan.

"There are only three ways a smart person can go broke: Liquor, Ladies and Leverage."

~Charlie Munger
Vice Chairman, Berkshire Hathaway

NOTES:

Conclusion

The book ends here, but your journey, dear reader, begins now. From Sunil, we learn that it is never too late to start.

One of the best things you can do for yourself is to work with and follow the Wealth Blueprint. It is the first step on the path to understanding what you must do with your assets, how you can best invest in your family's future, and prepare for a retired life without scaling back on your lifestyle.

Give at least half a day a month to go over your investments.

Keep track of your passive income. Take a pause when you're investing. Before you put money into anything, start the habit of writing down one page on why you must do this.

Understand and accept that investment appears to be a very boring and monotonous process because it keeps testing your patience. But just when you are about to give up on the market, it starts giving returns. So stick with the plan!

Need help?

Email book@naikwealth.in to book an appointment with me.

NOTES:

www.ingramcontent.com/pod-product-compliance
Lightning Source LLC
LaVergne TN
LVHW051301200726
843510LV00010B/1220